Edible Gifts

Edible Gifts

Kay Fairfax

photography by Martin Brigdale

RYLAND
PETERS
& SMALL

LONDON NEW YORK

Senior Designer Sally Powell

Commissioning Editor
Elsa Petersen-Schepelern

Production Deborah Wehner

Art Director Gabriella Le Grazie

Publishing Director Alison Starling

Food Stylist Kay Fairfax

Stylist Rebecca Duke

First published in the United States in 2001
by Ryland Peters & Small, Inc.,
519 Broadway, 5th Floor
New York, NY 10012
10 9 8 7 6 5 4 3 2 1
www.rylandpeters.com

Text © Kay Fairfax 2001.
Design and photographs © Ryland Peters & Small 2001

Printed and bound in China.

Library of Congress Cataloging-in-Publication Data

Fairfax, Kay.
  Edible gifts / Kay Fairfax ; photography by Martin Brigdale.
    p. cm.
  Includes index.
  ISBN 1-84172-182-4
  1. Cookery. 2. Gifts. I. Title.

TX652 .F34 2001
641.5--dc21   2001031856

STERILIZATION OF PRESERVING JARS

Wash the jars in hot, soapy water and rinse in boiling water. Place in a large saucepan and then cover with hot water. With the lid on, bring the water to the boil and continue boiling for 15 minutes. Turn off the heat, then leave the jars in the hot water until just before they are to be filled. Invert the jars onto a clean cloth to dry. Sterilize the lids for 5 minutes, by boiling, or according to the manufacturer's instructions. The jars should be filled and sealed while they are still hot.

The size and shape of jars are often dictated by the type of preserve you are making. Large jars with wide necks are needed for packing whole fruits, whereas smaller ones, 1–2 cups, are more useful for jellies, chutneys, or conserves.

All pickles and preserves should be processed in a boiling water-bath canner according to USDA guidelines. For information, see website http://hgic.clemson.edu/factsheets/HGIC3040.htm

Notes

All spoon measurements are level.

Preheat ovens to the specified temperature. Recipes in this book were tested with a convection oven. If using a regular oven, increase the cooking times according to the manufacturer's instructions.

Uncooked or partly cooked eggs should not be served to very young, old, or frail people, or to pregnant women.

Author's Acknowledgments

My special thanks to Elsa Petersen-Schepelern for her help and encouragement and to all the team at Ryland Peters & Small including designer, Sally Powell, Gabriella Le Grazie and Alison Starling, also to Rebecca Duke for her creative designing and ingenious packaging. To Clare Haynes and Sonia Brodie for their help with recipes and testing and to Janet Payne, Kay Partridge, Dimity Fairfax and to Pam Cooper for her fabulous friends. To my husband Michael Burton for putting up with kitchen chaos and most especially to Martin Brigdale for his generous hospitality and inspired photography.

contents

homemade delights

There is as much joy in making and giving handmade gifts as there is in receiving them. They do not need to be extravagant and expensive—people appreciate the time and thought that has gone into the gift far more than how much it has cost.

The recipes in this book do not have any added preservatives so will not keep as long as commercial varieties, but there is no comparison between the taste of fresh, natural ingredients and those bought from the supermarket.

You won't need any special equipment for the recipes and none is too difficult or demanding, but check before you start that you have appropriate containers on hand and how long a recipe will take to mature.

Containers don't have to be new and expensive and you can package your gift with flair and originality. There are edible gifts for all ages and tastes plus instructions and creative ideas for presentation.

The old adage "never judge a book by its cover" may still be true, but when it comes to giving and receiving, everyone loves a beautifully presented gift.

Sugar mice and coconut ice—plus chocolates and other candies—make perfect presents. We are never too young to start learning to

chocolates, candies, & fruits in liqueur

cook and a foolproof recipe for the children to start with is Coconut Ice. On the other hand we are never too old to enjoy the fruits of summer steeped in alcohol. So have fun with these recipes, but I suggest you make twice what you think you will need or you may not have anything left to give away.

9

Sugar mice are great fun—and not just for children. I made them one year for a St. Patrick's Day Dinner—colored green, they made pretty place card holders for guests to take home as a reminder of the evening.

sugar mice

5 cups confectioners' sugar, sifted

1 large egg white

1 tablespoon corn syrup

a few drops of red food coloring, enough to produce a pink mouse (optional)

decorations

silver or colored dragees for eyes

licorice strips or thin curled ribbon, for tails

Makes 10–12

Dust a work surface with a little of the confectioners' sugar.

Put the egg white into a large bowl and beat lightly until frothy. Add the corn syrup and stir with a wooden spoon until smooth. Add half the sifted confectioners' sugar, then, still using the wooden spoon, beat until smooth. Gradually add the remaining confectioners' sugar and food coloring, if using, and continue beating until all the sugar has been incorporated and the mixture is smooth. You may need to add a few drops of water if the mixture is too stiff.

Transfer to the dusted work surface and knead lightly until smooth and shiny. Divide the fondant mixture into 10–12 pieces. Cover with plastic wrap.

Working on one piece at a time, pinch off a small piece of fondant to make the ears and roll the remaining portion between the palms of your hand into the shape of a mouse. Divide the little piece of fondant in half and shape the 2 halves into ears. Make 2 small slits or holes in the head of the mouse and push in the ears. Carefully press silver or colored dragees into the face to make the eyes. Make a small hole for the tail, then take a thin strip of licorice or curling ribbon and push it into place.

Put the finished mice onto a flat tray lined with parchment paper. Cover with more of the parchment and let dry out completely in a warm spot for at least 2 days. Store in an airtight container for up to 6 months.

Note: Don't worry if the mice all look different, my first few attempts looked more like cats than mice, some were fat and others looked half starved. Others had very lopsided ears and a very cranky expression. It was rather fun to match them to the guests!

This old favorite sweetmeat is known in Turkey itself as *rahat lokum* and means "giving rest to the throat." Once you have mastered the basic technique, why not experiment with your own choice of flavors such as fresh ginger with orange or cinnamon with rosewater.

turkish delight

4½ tablespoons unflavored gelatin

3 cups sugar

1½ teaspoons rose water, or to taste

3–4 drops red food coloring

3 teaspoons cornstarch

3 cups confectioners' sugar

an 8-inch square cake pan, wetted with water

Makes about 64 pieces

Put 1¾ cups water in a heavy saucepan and bring to a boil. Reduce the heat, sprinkle in the gelatin, and stir with a metal spoon until the gelatin has melted. Add the sugar and stir continuously until dissolved.

Return to the boil and continue boiling for 10 minutes. Remove from the heat and stir in the rose water and food coloring.

Pour through a strainer lined with cheesecloth into the prepared cake pan and let cool. Let stand overnight to set.

Next day, sift the cornstarch and confectioners' sugar into a bowl, then sprinkle a thick layer onto a work surface. Transfer the remaining cornstarch-sugar mixture to a plastic bag.

Remove the Turkish Delight from the cake pan, loosening the edges if necessary with a wet knife and dipping the base of the pan into hot water for a few seconds. Turn out onto the coated work surface and cut into 1-inch strips each way, making 64 squares.

Put the squares in the plastic bag, together with any sugar left on the work surface, seal the bag and shake well until they are thickly and evenly coated.

Pack into an airtight container and sprinkle over any remaining sugar mixture.

VARIATIONS

Orange Nut Delight Instead of rose water and red food coloring, add 1 tablespoon strained orange juice, 1 tablespoon orange flower water, and 1 tablespoon ground crystallized orange rind at the same time as the sugar. Proceed as in the main recipe.

Lemon Nut Delight Omit the rose water and red food coloring. Stir in 1 tablespoon strained lemon juice. When the mixture is beginning to set, carefully stir through ⅓ cup blanched, chopped almonds or pistachios and proceed as in the main recipe.

chocolates, candies, and fruits in liqueur

This homemade recipe is much more delicious than the commercial variety—not nearly so sweet and very beautiful. It is incredibly easy to make, so no wonder it has always been a firm favorite with both children and adults.

coconut ice

7½ cups confectioners' sugar, sifted, plus extra for dusting

1 cup canned sweetened condensed milk

4¼ cups unsweetened desiccated coconut

2 tablespoons freshly squeezed lemon juice

3–4 drops vanilla extract

5–6 drops red food coloring

a rectangular pan, 11 x 7 x 2 inches, lined with parchment paper and lightly dusted with sifted confectioners' sugar

Makes about 40 pieces or 10 bars

Put the sifted confectioners' sugar into a large bowl, add the condensed milk and mix with a wooden spoon until smooth. Add the coconut, lemon juice, and vanilla and stir to form a stiff paste.

Spoon half the mixture onto the prepared pan and spread evenly over the base. Level the surface.

Add the red food coloring to the remaining mixture and stir well until the mixture turns pink. Spread evenly over the white layer.

Cover and let set, then cut into 2-inch squares with a small, sharp knife and package in wax-paper bags. Alternatively, cut in half crosswise across the rectangle, then in 5 strips lengthwise, giving 10 bars. Wrap in wax paper.

Coconut Ice will keep in an airtight container for about 2 weeks.

Note: When making chocolates, always buy the best brand of chocolate available and grate it or break it into small pieces before melting.

Chocolate should never come into contact with direct heat or water, so if possible use a double boiler. Excess heat, or even a drop of moisture will cause the chocolate to "seize"—become grainy—burn, or turn bitter, and there is no way to retrieve the mess.

Chocolate can also be melted in the microwave: consult the handbook before you start, use the lowest setting and stir and check about every 60 seconds.

Sweet truffles are supposed to look like the rare and elusive fungi of the same name—they are a traditional Christmas specialty in France. Homemade truffles have a much lighter, fresher taste than the commercial varieties and, if you hide them, will last several weeks in an airtight container in the refrigerator.

chocolate truffles

1¼ cups heavy cream

**1 lb. bittersweet chocolate
or couverture chocolate, grated**

1½ cups unsweetened cocoa powder, sifted

Makes about 50

Pour the cream into a heavy saucepan or the top of a double boiler and bring to a boil. Remove the pan from the heat and let cool until lukewarm. Add the grated chocolate and beat with an electric mixer for about 5 minutes. Set aside to cool, then beat the mixture for a further 5 minutes. Transfer the bowl to the refrigerator and chill for at least 10 minutes or until the mixture is firm enough to shape with your hands.

Sift the cocoa into a deep bowl or spread a thick layer on a baking sheet. Make sure your hands are clean and dry, then dust them with cocoa and, using about 2 heaped teaspoons of the mixture, quickly shape into a ball and roll in the cocoa. Put in little paper cases and store in airtight containers.

Coconut and Vanilla Truffles Add ½–1 cup unsweetened desiccated coconut and 1 tablespoon vanilla extract. Shape the mixture into small balls. Dip them into 1½ lb. melted chocolate and roll in cocoa as in the main recipe.

Rum-Raisin Truffles Add 2 tablespoons of rum and ½–1 cup seedless raisins. Shape the mixture into small balls and roll each one in chocolate threads or sprinkles, about 4 oz.

Coffee and Nut Truffles Add 2–3 tablespoons instant coffee granules to the hot cream, stir until dissolved, and proceed as in the main recipe. Pipe the mixture into small paper or foil confectionery cases and sprinkle with finely chopped nuts, about 1 cup.

chocolates, candies, and fruits in liqueur

Berries in liqueur taste as good as they look. Any combination of summer berries can be used, including fresh blackberries, blueberries, raspberries, boysenberries, and small strawberries. They make an unexpectedly colorful dessert in winter, served with whipped cream or crème fraîche, and are excellent used as an accompaniment to roast duck, chicken, or game. Best of all, you can drink the juice separately as a liqueur.

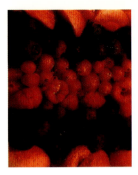

summer fruits in cointreau

6 cups berry fruits (a mixture of berries such as small strawberries, blueberries, raspberries, and others)

2 cups sugar

2 cups Cointreau or Grand Marnier

a 6-cup preserving jar, sterilized

Makes 6 cups

Wash, drain, and pat the berries dry with paper towels. Remove all leaves, stalks, or damaged pieces.

Arrange in layers about 1 inch deep in the sterilized glass jar, adding about 3 tablespoons sugar between each layer until the jar is full.

Pour in enough Cointreau or Grand Marnier to cover the fruit and fill the jar completely. Seal, label, and date and store in a cool, dark place for several months before using. Rotate the jar several times during storage to help the sugar dissolve.

Always choose figs of similar size: they must be firm and not overripe, otherwise when you prick them juice may seep out and discolor the liquid. You may prefer to use two smaller jars instead of one large one for a special gift.

figs in muscat

2–3 lb. firm, ripe figs, about 12–15

⅔ cup sugar

1¼ cups Muscat or port

a 6-cup preserving jar, sterilized

Makes 6 cups

Wipe the figs with a damp cloth and pat dry with paper towels. Trim the stalks and carefully prick the skins 5–6 times with a sterilized needle or toothpick.

Put the sugar and 1 cup water in a saucepan and stir over a low heat until the sugar is completely dissolved. Set aside to cool and stir in the Muscat or port. Carefully pack the figs into the prepared jar, without damaging the fruit, then pour in Muscat to cover the fruit and fill the jar completely. Seal, label, and date.

Store in a dark, cool place for several weeks before using.

The very small variety of pears, perfect for this recipe, are sometimes called Seckels, but if you have trouble finding them you can always use larger ones. If using a larger variety, peel, quarter, core, and remove the seeds and follow the recipe below.

tipsy pears

1 lb. small, firm ripe pears, about 8–10

1¼ cups red wine

1 cup sugar

1 cinnamon stick

½ cup brandy

a preserving pan

a 3-cup preserving jar, sterilized

Makes about 3 cups

Carefully wash and dry the pears, making sure the stalks are still attached. Put the Burgundy and sugar in a preserving pan or large saucepan and stir over a low heat until the sugar has completely dissolved.

Add the prepared pears and cinnamon stick to the syrup and bring to a boil. Reduce the heat and simmer until the pears are just tender, about 5 minutes. Remove the cinnamon stick and, using a slotted spoon, pack the pears into the prepared jar.

Return the syrup to the boil and boil rapidly without stirring for 5 minutes. Strain the syrup and add enough brandy to make 2½–3 cups of liquid, or enough to cover the pears completely.

Pour the syrup over the pears and top up the jars with more brandy if necessary. Seal, label, and date.

Store in a dark, cool place for at least 2 months before using.

All the recipes chosen for this section can be made a few days ahead and will still be fresh enough to give away—they are all easy to

cakes & cookies

package and transport. Why not try the Chinese fortune cookies for a children's party with appropriate jokes or, for your next dinner party, with fun messages in each one for the guests to read out?

Fortune cookies are not only delicious to eat but are great fun to make and to give to friends, especially at Christmas and New Year. The whole family can be involved making up jokes and fortunes or, if inspiration fails, you can buy great little books of funny quotes and sayings instead.

chinese fortune cookies

⅔ **cup all-purpose flour**

2 teaspoons ground ginger

3 large egg whites

1 cup confectioners' sugar, sifted

1 stick plus 1 tablespoon unsalted butter, melted

a 2-inch cookie cutter or glass

3–4 cookie sheets, greased and lightly floured

Makes about 18–20

Sift the flour and ginger into a small bowl. Put the egg whites into a large bowl and beat until just frothy. Add the confectioners' sugar and melted butter and beat until the mixture is smooth.

Beat in the flour and ginger mixture until the mixture forms a smooth paste, then set aside to rest for 15–20 minutes.

Using a cookie cutter or the edge of a glass, gently mark 6 circles about 2 inches in diameter on each cookie sheet. Working on one sheet at a time, put a heaped teaspoon of a mixture in the center of each circle. Smooth with a flat knife to fill each circle.

Bake in a preheated oven at 350°F for 6–7 minutes or until the edges start to brown. Remove the sheet from the oven and carefully and quickly slide each cookie onto a flat surface. Put a message in the center of each cookie and fold the cookie in half, then fold the 2 points towards each other—the dough is very pliable while still hot.

Continue baking and filling each cookie as they are ready—unless you have lots of helpers, you can only work on one sheet at a time, or the cookies will dry out before they can be folded.

Cool on a wire rack until completely dry. If packing in boxes to give as a gift, wrap in tissue paper first, so they won't break.

These little French cakes are delicious served for breakfast, afternoon tea, or with coffee after dinner. They are also perfect for using up leftover egg whites or frozen ones left over from an earlier recipe. Remember that if you are using frozen egg whites, they must be thawed to room temperature because chilled egg whites will not beat.

friands

1¾ sticks unsalted butter

1 cup plus 2 tablespoons confectioners' sugar, sifted, plus extra for dusting

⅓ cup all-purpose flour

1 cup ground almonds (or 1¼ cup slivered almonds, ground to a fine meal in a blender or food processor)

5 egg whites

1 tablespoon finely grated lemon or orange zest

12 small oval barquettes or dariole molds or mini loaf or muffin pans

a cookie sheet

Makes 12

Put the butter in a small saucepan and melt over a very low heat. Let cool. Brush the barquettes, molds, or pans with melted butter.

Sift the flour and confectioners' sugar together into a large bowl. Using a wooden spoon, stir in the ground almonds. Put the egg whites into a separate bowl and beat gently until light and frothy. Fold them through the dry ingredients.

Pour in the remaining melted butter and stir well. Stir in the lemon or orange zest.

Put the greased molds on a cookie sheet and fill each one three-quarters full with the mixture. Put the sheet onto the middle shelf of a preheated oven and bake at 400°F for 10 minutes, then turn them onto the sheet and bake for a further 7–10 minutes. They should be golden on top and firm to touch in the center.

Remove the sheet from the oven and let stand for about 5 minutes. Carefully invert each one onto a wire rack. When cool, dust generously with sifted confectioners' sugar, then store in an airtight container. Friands taste even better the next day and will last for at least 3 days stored this way.

Gingerbread with a difference. This is a delicious family favorite even without the frosting and with chocolate fudge frosting on top it makes a special gift. You can leave it whole as a large cake or cut into squares to be served as an after-dinner treat.

chocolate gingerbread

1 cup dark brown sugar

1 stick unsalted butter

1 cup corn syrup

2⅔ cups all-purpose flour

1½ teaspoons baking powder

½ teaspoon baking soda

2½ teaspoons ground ginger

1 egg, lightly beaten

⅔ cup whole milk

chocolate fudge frosting

1½ cups confectioners' sugar, sifted

¼ cup unsweetened cocoa powder, sifted

4 tablespoons unsalted butter, softened

1½ cups finely chopped nuts (optional)

a 9-inch square cake pan, greased and lined

Makes about 16

Put the sugar, butter, and corn syrup into a large saucepan. Heat gently over a low heat, stirring continuously, until the sugar has dissolved completely. Set aside to cool.

Sift the flour, baking powder, baking soda, and ground ginger into a bowl. Pour the cooled syrup over the dry ingredients and add the egg and milk. Stir until smooth.

Pour the mixture into the prepared cake pan and bake in a preheated oven at 300°F for 1¼–1½ hours, or until a skewer inserted in the center of the cake comes out clean. Let cool in the pan.

To make the frosting, put the confectioners' sugar, cocoa, and softened butter in a bowl and mix well. Gradually add a little hot water, 1 tablespoon at a time, mixing well, until the frosting is of a spreadable consistency. Spread the frosting evenly over the top of the cake and swirl gently with a fork. Sprinkle with chopped nuts if using and, when the frosting has set, cut into 2½-inch squares.

The original all-American brownie, with its rich, gooey texture, is a chocoholic's dream come true. You can add the chopped nuts to the mixture or sprinkle them over the frosting—either way is equally delicious.

chocolate brownies

1 stick plus 5 tablespoons unsalted butter

3 eggs

1⅓ cups sugar

¾ cup unsweetened cocoa powder, sifted, plus extra for dusting

½ teaspoon vanilla extract

½ cup all-purpose flour

8 oz. bittersweet chocolate, finely chopped or grated

1 cup nuts, such as walnuts, almonds, or pecans, coarsely chopped (optional)

chocolate cream

½ cup heavy cream

4 oz. finely chopped or grated bittersweet chocolate

a cake pan, 11 x 7 inches, lined with parchment paper extending 2 inches beyond the long ends

Makes about 15

Put the butter in a small saucepan and melt it slowly over a low heat.

Put the eggs in a bowl, beat lightly, then beat in the sugar. Stir in the melted butter, the cocoa, and vanilla. Using a wooden spoon or spatula, stir in the flour. Stir through the chopped chocolate and the nuts, if using.

Pour into the prepared cake pan and bake in a preheated oven at 325°F for about 25–30 minutes or until just firm in the center and still moist at the bottom. Do not overcook brownies, they are not meant to have the consistency of a cake and should be moist and gooey in the middle. They will dry out as they cool.

Remove from the oven and let stand, still in the pan, on a wire rack until completely cool.

Using the overhanging paper at the ends, carefully lift the brownie onto a board and peel off the paper. Dust with sifted cocoa or, for serious chocolate lovers, cover with chocolate cream and sprinkle with finely chopped nuts, if using. Cut into 2½-inch squares.

Chocolate Cream

Put the cream in a saucepan and heat until just simmering. Add the chocolate and stir until smooth and glossy. Transfer to the refrigerator for about 1 hour until the cream is firm enough to spread over the brownies.

How long do curds last? There's no need to worry, because once your

curds, butters, & conserves

family has tasted them, you'll be lucky if there are any left to give away. The jellies are so good you probably won't want to part with them either—even to your best friends. You don't need large amounts of these recipes, so keep small decorative jars to use and don't forget to sterilize them carefully before filling.

Hide this holiday treat as soon as you've made it or there'll be none left for Christmas Day and definitely none for New Years. It makes a fabulous present when accompanied by a box of homemade mini plum puddings or mince pies. The orange juice and grated zest mean that it's not as sweet as the usual brandy butter, and it's good enough to eat by the spoonful without the pudding or the mince pies. You can make a separate batch for the children, leaving out the brandy. If you want a larger amount, just double the recipe.

orange brandy butter

2½ sticks unsalted butter, softened

2½ cups confectioners' sugar, sifted

¼ cup ground almonds (or slivered almonds ground finely in a blender or food processor)

finely grated zest of 1 orange and 1 tablespoon strained freshly squeezed orange juice

1–2 tablespoons brandy

Makes about 4 cups, or 1¼ lb.

Put the butter and confectioners' sugar in a large bowl and beat until creamy. Add the ground almonds and beat again. Stir in the grated orange zest and strained juice, then the brandy.

The brandy butter will keep for several weeks in an airtight container in the refrigerator. It is very rich so it is better to package it in several small containers rather than one large one, unless it is for the family for Christmas.

Note: To prevent confectioners' sugar from becoming lumpy, keep it sealed in the refrigerator and sift as required.

A jelly that tastes as good as it looks—worth having in the pantry all year round. A traditional accompaniment for turkey, it is also good with roasted lamb.

cranberry jelly

4 lb. cranberries, fresh or frozen*

warmed sugar (see recipe)

a preserving pan

jelly bag or colander lined with 2 layers of cheesecloth

3 x 1-cup preserving jars, sterilized (see page 4)

Makes 3 cups

*Black or red currants may be used instead of the cranberries.

Wash and drain the berries. Put in a preserving pan or large saucepan with 4 cups water, bring to a boil, and simmer until soft, about 30 minutes. Mash them occasionally. Arrange a jelly bag or colander lined with a double layer of cheesecloth over a deep, non-metal container. Fill with the cranberry mixture and let the liquid drip through for several hours or overnight. Never be tempted to squeeze or stir the bag to hurry the process, or your jelly will be cloudy.

Next day, measure the liquid, then measure 2 cups sugar for every 2 cups of the liquid. Pour the liquid into a preserving pan. Bring slowly to a boil. Stir until the sugar has dissolved. Boil rapidly until setting point is reached, about 10 minutes (see page 38). Skim and pour into hot sterilized jars. Seal while hot. Label and date.

The jelly will keep for 6 months. It should be refrigerated after opening and used within 1 month.

A decorative and delicious jelly, very good with pork—once your friends taste it, they will be lining up for the recipe.

apple, mint, and peppercorn jelly

2 lb. green cooking apples, unpeeled

1 unwaxed lemon

**a small bunch of mint, plus
2 tablespoons chopped mint**

½ cup white wine vinegar

warmed sugar (see recipe)

**2 tablespoons bottled green
peppercorns, drained**

a preserving pan

*jelly bag or colander lined with
2 layers of cheesecloth*

*2 x 1-cup preserving jars, sterilized
(see page 4)*

Makes 2½ cups

Wash the apples and chop them into quarters. Wash the lemon and cut in half. Wash the mint thoroughly and shake off any excess water. Put the apples, lemon, bunch of mint, and vinegar in a preserving pan and add 2 cups water.

Bring to a boil, then reduce to a simmer and cook for 1 hour until the apples are soft—mash them occasionally with the back of a wooden spoon to help them break down. Arrange a jelly bag or a colander lined with a double layer of cheesecloth over a deep, non-metal container. Fill with the apple mixture and let the liquid drip through for several hours or overnight. Never be tempted to squeeze or stir the bag to hurry the process, or your jelly will be cloudy.

Next day, measure the liquid, then measure 2 cups sugar for every 2 cups of the liquid. Pour the liquid into a preserving pan. Bring slowly to a boil. Stir until the sugar has dissolved, then add the chopped mint and boil rapidly for 10 minutes or until setting point is reached (see page 38).

Bruise the peppercorns lightly and stir into the jelly. Let cool, stirring occasionally to make sure the mint and peppercorns are evenly distributed. Pour into hot, sterilized jars. Seal, label, and date.

The jelly will keep for 6 months. It should be refrigerated after opening and used within 1 month.

Curd makes an extra special gift if you also include a package of small meringues or mini pie shells. This may taste a little sweet when first made, but it will lose sweetness once it is cold. Also, it is well worth taking the time to strain the beaten eggs as there is often a surprising amount of residue left in the strainer.

grapefruit and lime curd

1 unwaxed grapefruit

2 unwaxed limes

4 large eggs

1½ cups sugar

3 x 1-cup preserving jars, sterilized

Makes about 3 cups

Wash and dry the fruit. Finely grate the zest of the grapefruit and 1 of the limes. Squeeze the juice, strain, and measure ¼ cup lime juice, and ½ cup grapefruit juice.

Put the eggs in a bowl and beat them lightly. Put the strained juices, grated zest, and sugar in the top of a double boiler, or a heatproof bowl set over a saucepan of simmering water. Stir.

Strain the beaten eggs into the mixture and stir over a very low heat until the sugar has dissolved and the mixture begins to thicken. Continue stirring until the mixture is thick enough to coat the back of a wooden spoon, about 20–40 minutes.

Pour the curd into hot, sterilized, dry jars. Cover, seal, label, and date. If unopened, this curd will keep for up to 8 weeks in the refrigerator. Use within 10–14 days of opening.

curds, butters, and conserves

A slightly richer and more creamy curd than the grapefruit recipe because it also includes butter. When filling glass containers with hot liquid always stand the warm jars on a damp cloth. This not only helps to stop them slipping but will also make sure they won't break.

lemon or lime curd

4 unwaxed limes or 2 large unwaxed lemons

4 large eggs

1 cup plus 2 tablespoons sugar

1 stick plus 2 tablespoons unsalted butter, softened

3 x 1-cup preserving jars, sterilized

Makes about 3 cups

Wash and dry the limes or lemons. Finely grate the zest and squeeze and strain the juice. Measure ½ cup juice and 1 tablespoon grated zest.

Put the eggs in a bowl and beat lightly.

Put the measured juice and zest, sugar, and butter in the top of a double boiler, or a heatproof bowl set over a saucepan of simmering water. Stir until the sugar has dissolved and the butter melted.

Strain the beaten eggs into the mixture and stir well. Continue to stir until the curd is thick enough to coat the back of a wooden spoon, at least 10 minutes, but up to 30 minutes.

Pour into hot, sterilized, dry jars. Cover, seal, label, and date.

This curd will keep, unopened, for up to 8 weeks in the refrigerator. Use within 10–14 days of opening. It is delicious as a spread on toast or in sandwiches, and for filling pies or cakes.

Take a day out with the family or friends and pick your own fresh fruit to make this jam. It's a fun way to spend a day and local or home-grown strawberries have so much more flavor and aroma than the commercial varieties.

strawberry jam

4 lb. strawberries

10 cups sugar (4 lb.)

juice of 4 lemons

1 teaspoon butter

peanut oil, for greasing

a preserving pan

4 x 2-cup preserving jars, sterilized

Makes about 8 cups

Wash the strawberries, pat dry with paper towels, then hull them. Grease a preserving pan lightly with the oil. Add the fruit, sugar, and lemon juice, stir well, then let stand for several hours until juices form.

Gradually bring to a boil stirring gently until the sugar has dissolved (about 10 minutes). Add the butter and boil until setting point is reached, about 2–5 minutes (see note below). Remove from the heat and skim the surface with a slotted spoon or fine strainer. Pour into hot, dry, sterilized jars. Seal, label, and date.

Setting Point: To test jams for setting, remove the pan from the heat. Take a small spoonful of the jam and put on a chilled plate. Let cool. Push it with your fingertip—if the jam is ready, the surface will set and wrinkle. If using a candy thermometer, warm it before putting it into hot jam. A good set should be assured when the temperature reaches 220°F. When setting point is reached, remove immediately from the heat because overboiling causes darkening and affects the consistency of the jam.

curds, butters, and conserves

Although you can now buy cherries all year round, for this recipe, wait until cherry season—they will be of better quality and much more reasonably priced.

cherry and orange jam

2 lb. pitted cherries, weighed after pitting, pits reserved

grated zest, freshly squeezed juice and pits of 1 large orange, about ¾ cup

freshly squeezed juice of 1 large lemon, about ⅓ cup

5 cups sugar

1 tablespoon slivered almonds

1 tablespoon Cointreau or Grand Marnier

a small cheesecloth bag

a preserving pan

3 x 2-cup preserving jars, sterilized

Makes about 6 cups

Put the cherry pits and orange pits in the cheesecloth bag and tie securely.

Put the fruit, zest, juices, and cheesecloth bag in a preserving pan or large saucepan. Simmer over a low heat until the cherries are soft. While the cherries are cooking, put the sugar in a baking pan in a preheated oven at 300°F for 10–15 minutes to heat through.

Remove the cheesecloth bag from the pan and slowly add the warm sugar. When the sugar has dissolved, increase the heat and boil rapidly until setting point is reached (see note page 38). Check after 10 minutes as this jam very quickly caramelizes. Remove the pan from the heat and carefully stir through the Cointreau or Grand Marnier and slivered almonds. Let cool slightly before bottling into hot sterilized jars. (If bottled while still hot the cherries and almonds will all rise to the surface.) Seal, label, and date.

curds, butters, and conserves

These flavored oils, scented with aromatic whole spices, chiles, and fresh herbs, will be a welcome addition to even the most

vinegars, oils, & olives

sophisticated cook's kitchen. Their looks belie how easy and inexpensive they are to make, but always use a good quality oil, preferably an extra virgin olive oil and not a bland non-specific vegetable variety. The same advice applies to the herbed olives: they must have good quality oil to bring out the best flavor.

Note: Sterilize attractively shaped jars or bottles which seal tightly and make sure the vinegar reaches the top of the bottle. Always let the vinegar cool completely before sealing.

If a cork is too large for the container, cut a wedge-shaped piece out of the end. The gap will close when pushed in.

Raspberry vinegar was indispensable in the Victorian pantry and is now in favor again. Flavored vinegars are perfect for deglazing the pan juices of roasted poultry, veal, or pork dishes. They also make a most refreshing summer drink—put about 1 tablespoon in a glass with ice and fill with sparkling water. A jigger of brandy makes them even more refreshing!

berry vinegar

3–6 cups raspberries, blackberries, or blueberries

4 cups white wine vinegar

sugar (see method)

2 x 2-cup bottles, sterilized

Makes 4 cups

Pick over the berries carefully, then put into a large jar or ceramic basin. Cover with the vinegar and let stand in a cool place for 7–10 days. Keep covered and stir gently every day.

After 10 days, pour through a fine nylon strainer or cheesecloth. Let drip but do not squeeze the fruit. Measure the vinegar, then measure 2½ cups sugar for every 2 cups liquid. Bring the vinegar gently to a boil, add the sugar, and simmer for 10 minutes. Skim if necessary. Let cool. Bottle and seal tightly before storing in a cool place. Use within 6–8 weeks.

lemon spice vinegar

2½ cups white wine vinegar

a small cinnamon stick, about 3 inches

2 small fresh bay leaves

zest of 1 lemon, removed in a long spiral

long spiral of fresh or dried orange zest the same size as the lemon

1 teaspoon black peppercorns

3 cloves

2–3 sprigs of lemon thyme

½ teaspoon coriander seeds

a 2½-cup bottle, with screw-top, stopper, or cork, sterilized

1 funnel

Makes 2½ cups

Put the vinegar in a saucepan and heat gently over a low heat. Add all the remaining ingredients and let steep in the pan until cool. Carefully poke the herbs and spices into the bottle and, using a funnel, pour in the vinegar.

Seal with a tight-fitting screw-top lid, stopper, or cork.

Place the bottle in a warm sunny position for 2–3 weeks to draw out the flavors. When the flavor is fully developed, remove the solids, strain, and rebottle. Store the vinegar in a cool dark place, then add fresh rind and a sprig of lemon thyme before giving as a gift. Use within 6–8 weeks.

Flavored vinegars are usually made from white wine or cider vinegar—and occasionally red wine or sherry vinegar. Always use a good quality variety with an acetic acid content of at least 5 percent and remember to leave enough time for the vinegar to stand for several weeks to mature before it will be ready to give away.

spicy mint vinegar

2 cups white wine vinegar

4 sprigs of fresh mint, 4–5 inches each

1 fresh bay leaf

½ teaspoon black peppercorns

3 dried red chiles

a 2-cup bottle, sterilized

Makes 2 cups

Put the vinegar in a stainless steel saucepan and warm over a low heat. Wash and dry the mint and bay leaf and coarsely crush the peppercorns. Put them into the prepared bottle, then add the chiles. Using a funnel, fill the bottle with the warmed vinegar. Let cool before sealing with a screw-top lid, stopper, or cork.

Put the bottle in a warm sunny position for 2–3 weeks to draw out the flavors. When the flavor is fully developed, remove the solids, strain, and rebottle. Store the vinegar in a cool dark place. Use within 6–8 weeks.

When giving it as a gift, add a fresh sprig of mint.

Flavored vinegar is ideal to use in salad dressings and this version will add a special piquancy to sauces, soups, and casseroles. It is also particularly good to add to marinades and to deglaze pans after cooking meat, fish, and poultry.

chile vinegar

2 cups white or red wine vinegar

2–3 fresh bay leaves

4–6 small red chiles, fresh or dried

a 2-cup bottle, sterilized

Makes 2 cups

Put the vinegar in a stainless steel saucepan and warm over a low heat. Wash and dry the bay leaves and fresh chiles.

Put the bay leaves, chiles, and garlic in the prepared bottle and fill with the warmed vinegar. Let cool before sealing with a tight fitting screw-top lid, stopper, or cork. Use within 6–8 weeks.

Proceed as for Spicy Mint Vinegar, adding a fresh chile and fresh bay leaf to give as a gift.

vinegars, oils, and olives

This is a delightful piquant oil and is the perfect partner for a green summer salad and wonderful for basting roasted duck.

orange and saffron oil

5–7 long thin strips of fresh or dried orange peel

½–1 teaspoon saffron threads

1 teaspoon coriander seeds, bruised

a sprig of rosemary, about 5 inches

olive oil

a 2–2½-cup bottle, sterilized

Makes 2–2½ cups

Put the orange peel, saffron, coriander seeds, and rosemary sprig into a prepared glass bottle. Using a funnel, add enough olive oil to fill the bottle.

Seal tightly and store in a cool dark place for 2 weeks before using.

A very useful oil to keep in the pantry: try stirring a few tablespoons through hot pasta with a handful of freshly chopped herbs and grated Parmesan cheese—or use it in the wok with your next stir-fry.

chile oil

3 fresh bay leaves

6 fresh small red chiles

1 teaspoon whole black peppercorns

olive oil

a 2–2½-cup bottle, sterilized

Makes 2–2½ cups

Wash and dry the bay leaves and chiles. Put all the ingredients in the prepared glass bottle and, using a funnel, fill the bottle with olive oil. Remember to leave enough room at the top if you are using a cork or stopper instead of a screw-top lid.

Store in a cool dark place for at least 2 weeks before using.

vinegars, oils, and olives

Herbs should be picked early in the morning before the sun vaporizes their oils: always choose fresh young growth that hasn't yet flowered as the flavor is more intense. The sprigs should be about 6 inches long.

green herb oil

a sprig of tarragon

a sprig of rosemary

a sprig of sage

a sprig of thyme

3 small fresh bay leaves

1 teaspoon whole black or red peppercorns

olive oil

a 2–2½ cup bottle, sterilized

Makes 2–2½ cups

Wash and dry the herbs and push them into a prepared glass bottle. Add the peppercorns. Using a funnel, fill the bottle with olive oil and seal with a tightly fitting non-corrosive screw-top lid, stopper, or cork.

Store in a cool dark place for at least 1 week before using.

Note: Oils do not last forever and those containing fresh herbs are best used within 3 months of making. The ingredients for the recipes on these 2 pages are enough to fill a bottle of 2–2½ cup capacity, but try using 2 smaller bottles so that they will be used more quickly.

vinegars, oils, and olives

The flavorful marinating oil from these olives is delicious—use it separately in cooking or on salads. You can top up the oil and the olives as they are used.

balsamic and oregano olives

1 lb. good-quality black or green olives, such as kalamata or picholine

6 tablespoons olive oil

2 tablespoons balsamic vinegar

1 fat garlic clove, chopped

1 teaspoon chopped oregano

a wide-necked glass jar with a non-metallic lid, about 2 cups, sterilized

Makes about 2 cups

Rinse the olives and leave to drain on paper towels.

Put all the ingredients into the sterilized jar and seal. Gently shake or turn the jar upside down a few times to coat the olives.

Let stand in a cool place for a least 2 days before serving, then use within 1 month.

Once opened, keep stored in the refrigerator and remember to remove 30 minutes before serving.

According to your choice of herbs, these olives could have an interesting effect if eaten in great quantities: cilantro, for instance, was used in the Middle Ages as an aphrodisiac and thyme was taken as part of a ritual to enable one to see fairies.

green olives with cilantro and thyme

1 lb. green olives, such as picholine, rinsed and drained

1 teaspoon black peppercorns, crushed

1 fat garlic clove, finely chopped, not crushed

3–4 small strips of lemon peel

¼ cup finely chopped cilantro and thyme leaves

olive oil, to cover

2 wide-necked glass preserving jars, 1¼ cups each, sterilized

Makes about 2½ cups

Put all the ingredients, except the oil, in the jars.

Fill the jars with the oil until all the olives are covered. Shake gently to mix.

Store in a cool place and let marinate for 1 week or 10 days, then use within 1 month.

Most fresh herbs can be used in this recipe, but the basic varieties are thyme and parsley. Don't use basil as it can turn black in oil.

stuffed olives with fresh herbs

3 tablespoons olive oil

¼ cup finely chopped fresh herbs

1 large garlic clove, finely chopped, not crushed

1 teaspoon black peppercorns, crushed

3–4 small strips of fresh lemon zest

8 oz. stuffed green olives, rinsed and drained

a 1¼-cup preserving jar, sterilized

Makes about 1¼ cups

Put the oil, herbs, garlic, peppercorns, and lemon zest into a bowl and mix well. Add the olives and stir gently until they are all well coated with oil.

Transfer to the prepared jar, seal, and store in the refrigerator. Shake the jar occasionally to move the olives around.

They can be eaten after 24 hours and will keep for about 1 month.

chutneys, relishes, & mustards

These are much loved, classic gifts that everyone enjoys. Such is the variety of ingredients for chutneys, relishes, and mustards, that they can be made all year round and will keep for ages. When making a batch always hide a few extra jars in your pantry and you will never be caught short for want of a small gift for that unexpected occasion.

It is impossible to give exact quantities for many of these recipes, as it depends on how juicy your fruit and vegetables are and exactly what size jars you have. However, I have suggested amounts that will make good gifts. This relish is not only decorative, but it will also enhance any roasted meat, poultry, or game dishes.

red bell pepper relish

2 cucumbers, about 8 inches each, peeled, seeded, and diced

4 onions, 2 red and 2 white, sliced

4 celery stalks, chopped

2 large garlic cloves, finely crushed (optional)

2 large red bell peppers, seeded and finely chopped

2 large green bell peppers, seeded and finely chopped

⅓ cup salt, preferably sea salt

1¾ cups cider or white wine vinegar

1 teaspoon mustard seeds

1½ cups sugar

½ teaspoon ground allspice

½ teaspoon fennel seeds

2 x 1¼-cup preserving jars, sterilized

Makes 2½ cups

Put all the vegetables into large bowl, sprinkle with the salt, cover, and refrigerate overnight.

Next day, drain, pressing to get rid of the liquid. Put into a plastic strainer and rinse with cold running water. Drain again, then press with paper towels to dry off as much as possible. Set aside.

Put all the remaining ingredients into a saucepan and bring to a boil. Add the drained vegetables and return to a boil. Simmer for 30 minutes or until the vegetables are just tender.

Spoon the mixture into the prepared jars. Seal tightly, label, and date.

Store for 3 months before eating. After opening, keep the jars covered in the refrigerator and use the relish within 2–3 weeks.

chutneys, relishes, and mustards

A relish with a delicious tropical flavor—don't be afraid to try different combinations. Use other fruits if you can't find tropical varieties, and maybe add a few raisins.

summer fruit relish

1 small ripe mango, peeled and chopped fairly small

1 small papaya, peeled and chopped fairly small

2 onions, peeled and finely sliced

about 20 pitted dried dates, chopped

2 large guavas, peeled and chopped fairly small, or the pulp and seeds of 6 passionfruit

2 medium baking apples, peeled, cored, and chopped

2–3 fresh apricots, pitted and chopped

1½ cups white wine vinegar or cider vinegar

2 cups sugar

2 tablespoons sea salt

½ inch fresh ginger, peeled and grated

6 juniper berries, slightly crushed, or 1 teaspoon powdered allspice

1 heaped tablespoon freshly ground black pepper

a preserving pan

2 x 2¼-cup preserving jars, sterilized

Makes about 5½ cups

Put all the ingredients into a preserving pan or large, heavy saucepan. Heat slowly, stirring until the sugar has dissolved. Bring to a boil and simmer for about 1 hour 40 minutes or until very thick. Spoon into hot sterilized jars and cover with plastic-coated lids. Keep for 3 months before opening. After opening, keep covered in the refrigerator and use within 2–3 weeks.

These chiles are so decorative I always have a jar on show in my kitchen, even if I never open it.

pickled chiles

about 1½ lb. red serrano chiles, about 2 inches long

1 cup white wine vinegar

1 cup sugar

½ teaspoon sea salt

2 x 2-cup preserving jars, sterilized

Makes about 4 cups

Thoroughly wash and drain the chiles. Leave them whole or halve them lengthwise and remove the seeds if you prefer.

Put them in a saucepan with the vinegar, sugar, and salt. Bring to a boil and let simmer until the sugar has dissolved and the chiles are tender, about 6–8 minutes.

Remove from the heat and let cool before packing into the sterilized jars. Seal tightly, label, and date, then store in the refrigerator. Leave for 2 weeks before using. After opening, keep covered in the refrigerator and use within 2–3 weeks.

Note: Remember when handling chiles, either wear gloves, or use tongs or a knife and fork, and keep your hands well away from your eyes.

A perfect gift for friends who enjoy hot and spicy flavors.

preserved sweet chiles

4 oz. medium to large fresh red chiles

2¼ cups sugar

1¾ cups white wine vinegar

2 preserving jars, 1 cup each, sterilized

Makes 2 cups

Slice the chiles crosswise into 1-inch pieces. Rinse well and drain, removing as many seeds as possible for a less fiery flavor. Put the chiles and sugar into a heavy saucepan and add the vinegar. Bring slowly to a boil, then let simmer until the chiles are tender, about 5–7 minutes. Remove from the heat and let cool. Spoon into the prepared jars, seal tightly, label, and date.

Store in a cool, dark place for 2 weeks before using. After opening, keep covered in the refrigerator and use within 2–3 weeks.

chutneys, relishes, and mustards

55

A special homemade gift for Christmas or Thanksgiving, this chutney can be made at least a month in advance and, being a cooked variety, it will keep for several months if stored in a cool, dark, dry place. It is very colorful and decorative and is the perfect accompaniment for turkey and ham, hot or cold poultry, salads, and cheese. Try your hand at making your own labels—they are very easy to create on a computer and lend that extra personal touch to the gift.

cranberry and raisin chutney

4 cups fresh or frozen cranberries

½ cup white wine vinegar or cider vinegar

½ cup seedless raisins

⅔ cup chopped nuts (Brazil nuts or almonds are best)

finely grated zest and juice of 2 lemons

½ teaspoon ground ginger

½ teaspoon paprika

½ teaspoon ground cinnamon

½ teaspoon sea salt

2 cups sugar

a preserving pan

4 x 1-cup preserving jars, sterilized

Makes 4 cups

Put all the ingredients, except the cranberries, into a preserving pan or heavy stainless steel saucepan. Add ¾ cup water, bring to a boil, reduce the heat, and simmer until tender. Add the cranberries and simmer for 40 minutes or until the fruit is soft but not disintegrated, about 45 minutes.

Spoon into the prepared jars. Cover and seal tightly, label, and date. Store in a cool dark place for 2–3 weeks before using. After opening, use within 3 months.

Delicious with hot or cold roast pork, lamb, broiled fish, and curries.

gingered banana chutney

1 lb. onions, 3 medium, coarsely chopped

2 cups coarsely chopped dried dates

2 garlic cloves, coarsely chopped

1½ lb. bananas, weighed after peeling

1¾ cups malt vinegar

1½ cups seedless raisins

2 inches fresh ginger, peeled and finely chopped

1 cup pineapple juice

juice of 2 lemons, about ½ cup

1 tablespoon mustard seeds

1 teaspoon sea salt

3 whole cloves

Tabasco sauce, to taste

3 x 1-cup preserving jars, sterilized

Makes 3 cups

Put the onions, dates, and garlic in a heavy stainless steel saucepan. Add the mashed bananas and vinegar. Bring to a boil, cover, and simmer for about 20 minutes.

Add the raisins, ginger, fruit juices, and spices. Bring to a boil and simmer for 10–15 minutes, stirring constantly until the mixture is thick. Add Tabasco to taste. Pour into hot, sterilized jars. Cool, seal, label, and date.

Store in the refrigerator for 2 days before using. Most chutneys improve by storing for 2–3 weeks before using: this one can be eaten after 2–3 days.

Perfect to serve with hot or cold poultry, salads, or a mature cheese.

peach chutney

1 onion, chopped

3 cups seedless raisins, chopped

1 garlic clove, chopped

4½ lb. peaches, peeled, pitted, and diced

2 inches fresh ginger, peeled and chopped

2 tablespoons chile powder

2 tablespoons mustard seeds

1 tablespoon salt, preferably sea salt

4 cups cider vinegar

4 cups soft brown sugar

5 x 2-cup preserving jars, sterilized

Makes about 10 cups

Put all the ingredients into a heavy stainless steel or enamel saucepan. Bring to a boil. Stir, reduce the heat, and simmer for about 1 hour.

Pour into hot sterilized jars. Cover, seal, label, and date. Store for 4 weeks before using.

Now you don't have to serve both mustard and horseradish sauce with the roast beef as this delicious variety combines both flavors. As a gift, fill several small decorative jars or pots and attach a small mustard spoon.

horseradish mustard

1 cup dry mustard powder

⅓ cup horseradish. freshly grated or bottled

1 teaspoon sea salt

¼ cup extra virgin olive oil

½ cup cider vinegar

1 tablespoon honey

1 tablespoon freshly squeezed lemon juice

3 small ½-cup preserving jars, sterilized

Makes about 1½ cups

Put all the ingredients in a blender and process for 30 seconds or until the mixture is smooth and creamy.

Ladle into small attractive glass jars and seal tightly.

Store in the refrigerator for 1 week to 10 days before using, and eat within 3 months of opening. After opening, keep covered in the refrigerator and use within 1 month.

This mustard smells and tastes wonderful. It is quite spicy, but sweeter than most and it mellows with age. Once opened, mustard must be kept in the refrigerator and eaten within about a month.

sweet cardamom mustard

⅓ cup mustard seeds

2 tablespoons dry mustard powder

1 teaspoon sea salt

½ teaspoon ground turmeric

10–12 cardamom pods

5–6 green peppercorns

1 teaspoon freshly grated nutmeg

¼ cup red wine

¼ cup cider vinegar

1 tablespoon honey

2 small ½-cup preserving jars, sterilized

Makes about 1 cup

Coarsely grind the mustard seeds with a mortar and pestle or clean coffee grinder. Transfer to a bowl, then stir in the mustard powder, salt, turmeric, and nutmeg.

Remove the seeds from the cardamom pods and crush with the peppercorns, using the back of a spoon, a rolling pin, or a mortar and pestle. Add to the mustard and stir well.

Stir in the wine, vinegar, and honey until well blended and thick. If it is too thick add a little more wine or vinegar.

Cover the bowl and let stand for about 12 hours before spooning into small glass jars. Seal tightly and store for 3–4 weeks before using. After opening, keep covered in the refrigerator and use within 1 month..

chutneys, relishes, and mustards

61

Bouquet garni is the classic bundle of fresh, aromatic herbs used to flavor casseroles, soups, and stock. The kitchen twine makes it easier to remove after cooking—lots of flavor and no mess!

bouquet garni

1–2 fresh bay leaves

sprigs of parsley

sprigs of thyme

Your choice of:

3-inch piece of celery stalk

sprigs of rosemary, lemon thyme, tarragon, or other herbs

Makes 1 bouquet garni

Tie the herbs together with kitchen twine, leaving a long loop of string to tie the bouquet to the handle of the pot—this makes it easier to remove from the finished dish. Alternatively, put the loose herbs in a double thickness of cheesecloth. Secure tightly with twine, leaving the twine long as before.

Bouquet garni can be made from dried or powdered herbs, but they are no substitute for the fresh version.

Note: Fresh herbs, especially those with soft leaves, such as basil or parsley, wilt quickly. Assemble just before presenting the gift.

A new and different bouquet garni—these traditional herbs from Thailand turn an ordinary dish into an extraordinary one. Compose at the last minute because cilantro wilts quickly.

Thai-style bouquet garni

I inch fresh ginger, sliced

a few sprigs of cilantro

I red chile, preferably Thai

Your choice of:

I stalk of lemongrass

a sprig of kaffir lime leaves or a piece of lime zest

sprigs of Thai mint or basil

Makes I bouquet garni

Put the ginger, cilantro, and chile in a bundle, then add your choice of other ingredients. If using lemongrass, split it lengthwise. Arrange all ingredients in a bundle and tie up with kitchen twine. Use immediately.

index

conversion charts

Weights and measures have been rounded up or down slightly to make measuring easier.

VOLUME EQUIVALENTS:

American	Metric	Imperial
1 teaspoon	5 ml	
1 tablespoon	15 ml	
¼ cup	60 ml	2 fl.oz.
⅓ cup	75 ml	2½ fl.oz.
½ cup	125 ml	4 fl.oz.
⅔ cup	150 ml	5 fl.oz. (¼ pint)
¾ cup	175 ml	6 fl.oz.
1 cup	250 ml	8 fl.oz.

WEIGHT EQUIVALENTS:

Imperial	Metric
1 oz.	25 g
2 oz.	50 g
3 oz.	75 g
4 oz.	125 g
5 oz.	150 g
6 oz.	175 g
7 oz.	200 g
8 oz. (½ lb.)	250 g
9 oz.	275 g
10 oz.	300 g
11 oz.	325 g
12 oz.	375 g
13 oz.	400 g
14 oz.	425 g
15 oz.	475 g
16 oz. (1 lb.)	500 g
2 lb.	1 kg

MEASUREMENTS:

Inches	Cm
¼ inch	5 mm
½ inch	1 cm
¾ inch	1.5 cm
1 inch	2.5 cm
2 inches	5 cm
3 inches	7 cm
4 inches	10 cm
5 inches	12 cm
6 inches	15 cm
7 inches	18 cm
8 inches	20 cm
9 inches	23 cm
10 inches	25 cm
11 inches	28 cm
12 inches	30 cm

OVEN TEMPERATURES:

225°F	110°C	Gas ¼
250°F	120°C	Gas ½
275°F	140°C	Gas 1
300°F	150°C	Gas 2
325°F	160°C	Gas 3
350°F	180°C	Gas 4
375°F	190°C	Gas 5
400°F	200°C	Gas 6
425°F	220°C	Gas 7
450°F	230°C	Gas 8
475°F	240°C	Gas 9